Stalking

Elaine Landau

Franklin Watts

A Division of Grolier Publishing
New York / London / Hong Kong / Sydney
Danbury, Connecticut

For Michael

Interior design by Molly Heron
Photographs ©: Ben Klaffke: 6, 10, 17, 35, 39, 40, 44, 46,
51, 57, 60, 64, 66, 73, 76, 78, 82; Reuters/Bettmann: 24,
31, 32; UPI/Bettmann: 22.

Landau, Elaine.
Stalking / by Elaine Landau.
p. cm.
Includes index.
Summary: Charts the growing awareness of this crime and
explores such areas as the connection between stalking and
domestic violence, antistalking legislation, and what victims
can do to protect themselves.
ISBN 0-531-11295-0
1. Stalking—Juvenile literature. [1. Stalking.] I. Title.
HV6594.L36   1996
364.1'5—dc20   96-5088
                                        CIP
                                        AC

Contents

Two coworkers enjoy lunch together. As Laura Black found, sometimes a casual outing can be viewed by a potential stalker as a romantic encounter.

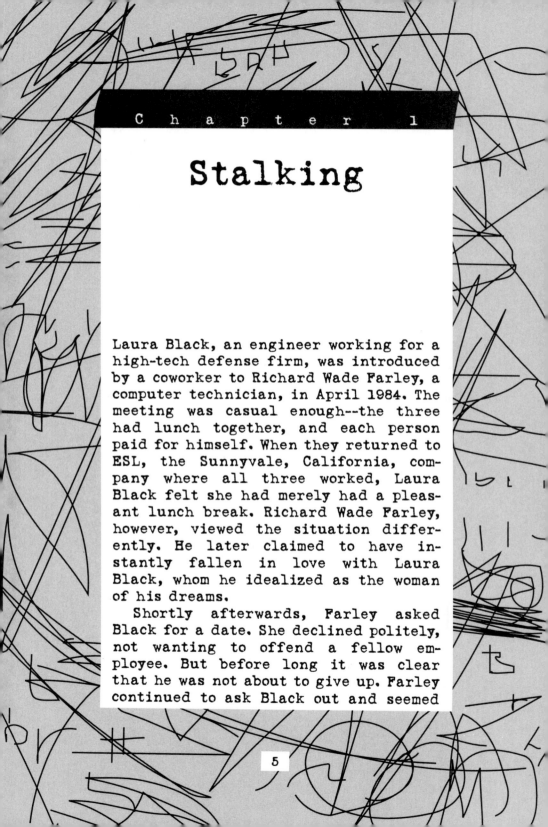

Stalking

Laura Black, an engineer working for a
high-tech defense firm, was introduced
by a coworker to Richard Wade Farley, a
computer technician, in April 1984. The
meeting was casual enough--the three
had lunch together, and each person
paid for himself. When they returned to
ESL, the Sunnyvale, California, company where all three worked, Laura
Black felt she had merely had a pleas-
ant lunch break. Richard Wade Farley,
however, viewed the situation differ-
ently. He later claimed to have in-
stantly fallen in love with Laura
Black, whom he idealized as the woman
of his dreams.

Shortly afterwards, Farley asked
Black for a date. She declined politely,
not wanting to offend a fellow employee. But before long it was clear
that he was not about to give up. Farley
continued to ask Black out and seemed

shocked that she always turned him down. Attempting to win Black over, he sent her a duck-shaped planter and a decorative mirror along with an assortment of other gifts. In return for his adoration, Farley kept insisting that Black give him her address and home phone number.

But Laura Black wasn't flattered by Farley's attention. Instead, she felt he had invaded her privacy. When her tactful refusals didn't deter him, Black finally told Farley that she wouldn't go out with him if he were the last man on earth.

Yet Richard Wade Farley showed no sign of giving up. As he subsequently explained his reasoning, "I had the right to ask her out. She had the right to refuse. When she did not refuse in a cordial way, I felt I had the right to bother her."[1] Bothering Laura Black took the form of frightening intrusions into her personal life. Besides secretly making copies of her home and office keys, Farley secured access to Black's personnel file to obtain her date of birth, home address, and phone number.

Shortly thereafter, Farley began tailing Laura Black with the zeal of a private detective. He would follow her home from work, park in front of her house, and take down the license plate numbers of her male suitors. He habitually parked behind a convenience store where Laura Black shopped, and he joined Black's health club. Farley also attended company softball games in which she played. Laura Black moved three times hoping to lose him, but Farley always found out were she lived.

Richard Wade Farley's obsession with Laura Black continued for years. He continually wrote to her, taking up to eight hours to compose a letter. Frequently, he enclosed pictures he had drawn of her wearing a leotard. He indicated that he wanted to purchase a home with Black and even suggested that they see a marriage counselor because, he told her, "we fight like an old married couple."[2] Sometimes Farley used his letters to manipulate Black. He would set a day and time for a date and write that if she didn't respond he would assume she had agreed. When on one occasion she failed to reply, he showed up at her door dressed in a suit for dinner.

Their employer, ESL, warned Farley that he would be fired if he didn't stop harassing Black. But Farley couldn't break free of his obsession. "I was hooked on her," he recalls. "I had fallen madly in love with her and I had to see her, even if I had to make her mad."[3]

In addition to making Laura Black "mad," Farley continued to frighten her. In a letter to her, he described the possible effect of his potential loss of employment:

> Once I'm fired, you won't be able to control me ever again. Pretty soon I'll crack under the pressure and run amok and destroy everything in my path. . . . The newspaper people will hound you. Even if you don't crack up, you will never again play with men with the same ease that you do now, and I will win.[4]

Following Farley's dismissal from ESL in May 1986, he continued to call Laura Black at work as well as write to her. Sensing he might never win her over, Farley's correspondence became especially desperate and threatening. "I do own guns, and I'm good with them," he wrote. "I'm really not insane, but I'm calculating. I just might scare us both with what I might do if I'm pushed into it."[5] Months later in another letter, he noted, "You cost me my job. . . . Yet I still like you. . . . Why do you want to find how far I'll go? Is it so that you can be right and win? Don't consider me a joke. I absolutely will not be pushed around, and I'm beginning to get tired of being nice."[6]

Unfortunately, stalking situations can arise
in the workplace, making it very difficult
for the victim to avoid the pursuer.

Although Richard Wade Farley got a job at another
firm, and even began steadily dating another woman,
his interest in Laura Black never waned. In response,
Black went to court to secure a temporary restraining
order against him. The judge ordered him to stay at

least 300 yards (274 m) from Black's home, office, and gym. The judge also set a hearing date for Black to obtain a permanent restraining order.

At this point, Farley felt as though his world were crumbling. On the day prior to the hearing for the permanent restraining order, he bought a 12-gauge semi-automatic shotgun and filled a rented motor home with nearly one hundred rounds of ammunition. He then put on army fatigues and a headband before heading for ESL to confront Laura Black. Looking back on that day, Farley claims that at first he had only intended to talk Black out of going for the restraining order. If he failed to do so, Farley planned to shoot up the ESL computers before killing himself in front of Black. "I just felt she had to see the end result of what I felt she had done to me," Farley recalls. "It was important to me that she saw it and not just read about it."[7]

But this is not how things turned out. As Richard Wade Farley entered ESL to see Black, he began shooting at nearly everyone he passed on the way to her office. Farley came prepared for his gruesome mission. He had draped himself with an assortment of weapons, including a knife, a semiautomatic shotgun, a .357 magnum revolver, and a .22 magnum revolver. As his gunfire sounded through the second floor, smoke, screams, and spattered blood seemed to be everywhere. Before surrendering to the police and SWAT team that arrived, Farley killed seven people and wounded four others. Among the injured was Laura Black. She was shot in the shoulder and had to undergo seven operations to repair the damage to her body. Nevertheless, at his trial Farley referred to his imagined love relationship with her in the present tense.

Another young woman who has been hounded by a potentially deadly stalker is Kathleen Baty. The trouble started in 1982 when she was a college student at UCLA and had come home for Thanksgiving vacation. A man telephoned her at her parents' residence. He told her that he had been in a physical education class with her at the junior college Baty had attended before going to UCLA. Baty knew this wasn't true—she had been on a track scholarship and hadn't taken physical education. She felt the phone call becoming "kind of weird" and she hung up—but the caller's voice, and his distinctive speech impediment, seemed familiar. Later, she saw a former high school classmate in a parked car next to hers, and she realized the man was the caller. His name was Larry Stagner. As he drove away, Baty noticed that he had a semiautomatic weapon in the back of his pickup truck.

The next day, when Larry Stagner called Baty a second time, she hung up on him again. He called the day after that, and again she hung up. Soon, Baty didn't feel comfortable even answering the phone, but Stagner was persistent—calling every five minutes for up to four hours. One night, as Baty returned from a date, Larry Stagner jumped out from the bushes behind her with a knife. Her date chased him away, but soon afterwards he was spotted circling Kathleen Baty's house in his car. Stagner later called her home with this threat: "Tell the big guy [Kathleen's date] I'm going to kill him. I have 180 rounds of ammunition and am going to blow him away."[8] By then the police had been contacted, and when Stagner drove by again, they chased him across the city before finally apprehending him. He was jailed for forty-eight hours on a psychiatric hold and then released.

Ms. Baty did not hear from Stagner again until February 1983. While she was visiting her parents for the weekend, Larry Stagner unexpectedly appeared at their front door. Kathleen wasn't home at the time, but upon her return she found police surrounding the house. The officers remained with Kathleen and her parents until the family's next contact with Stagner—he telephoned at 2:00 A.M. The officers traced the call, and as before, they had to engage in a car chase to catch him. When captured, he had semiautomatic weapons in his possession. He also told police of an elaborate plan to kidnap Kathleen Baty and take her up to the Sierra Nevada mountains. This time, Larry Stagner served sixty days in jail and was required to be an outpatient at a mental institution for a year.

Kathleen Baty's next encounter with Stagner occurred in May 1986 after she had graduated from college and was residing in Marina del Ray, a southern California beach community. After Baty had been away for a week, a neighbor told her that a man had attempted to break into her apartment. Although some neighbors tried to catch him, he got away. When Kathleen Baty showed her a newspaper clipping of Larry Stagner, the woman identified him as the culprit.

This was just the start of things to come. Apparently, Stagner had been watching Baty's oceanfront apartment complex for a while. The next day, as Baty walked back from the beach, she spotted him coming towards her through a small alleyway. Pretending she hadn't seen him, Baty ran to her apartment and dialed 911. Meanwhile, Stagner returned to his car, got a gun, and headed for Baty's apartment.

Hoping to escape, Baty quickly jumped over the divider separating her patio from her neighbor's residence. She made it, but unfortunately she impaled her leg on a wrought iron planter hook in the process. She describes the resulting chaotic scene as follows:

> We're [her roommate, her neighbor, and herself] screaming and the police—I had given the police his license plate number because I could see it—and the police came in full force. . . . It was at the

beach, so they were all on their bikes, their Broncos, or whatever. And we looked down and everyone's screaming and he [Stagner] heard us all scream and he got in his car and he drove right past them. Got away.[9]

By this time, Kathleen Baty's encounters with Larry Stagner had begun to take a toll on her. She remembers, "As it got worse and worse, I kept saying, you know, 'This guy's not going away.' And I started to have dreams and nightmares and the whole bit."[10] Trying not to allow it to affect her life, Baty met and married her husband and moved to Menlo Park in northern California. As her husband was a professional football player, however, Baty was frequently home alone. While alone, she often received telephone calls from Stagner.

By January 1990, she began seeing him parked outside her home again. Stagner was arrested and jailed for four months. But the situation worsened once he was released. The day after Stagner's release, Baty received a call from his probation officer. He told her, "Be on the lookout. He was just released from jail and he gave us a phony address and phone number, and I think he's coming after you."[11]

The probation officer was right. One afternoon, Baty entered her house to find Stagner waiting for her with a knife in his hand. Luckily, while she was trying to calm him, her mother called and pieced together what was going on. Baty's mother said she would call the police, but by the time Stagner had bound Baty's hands and led her, now at gunpoint, to his car, there was still no one in sight. Baty describes what happened next: "We walked out. He put the gun behind him and the keys in the car door. . . . I saw no one because everyone was hidden. . . . And [then] police from everywhere said 'Freeze!'"[12]

Baty escaped, but Larry Stagner held the police at bay for eleven hours. Once arrested and convicted, he was sentenced to eight years and ten months in prison with the possibility of parole in four years. Although he had tormented Baty for years, he received a lesser sentence because he was charged with attempted kidnapping rather than kidnapping. This is because kidnapping technically involves moving the victim a predetermined number of feet. Stagner had stopped just short of the required distance when the police interrupted his scheme.

Although Kathleen Baty and Laura Black had to endure harrowing ordeals, they survived. Not everyone in similar situations is as fortunate. This is the case with Caroline Witt, a twenty-two-year-old from Crystal Lake, Illinois, who was repeatedly harassed by her former boyfriend Kristoffer Wendt. Witt tried to tell him that their relationship was over, but he refused to accept it. Wendt continually called the young woman, wrote her notes, and even left flowers on her car. When he couldn't win her back, Wendt told her, "If I can't have you, no one can."[13]

Wendt's irrational pursuit of his former girlfriend came to a horrifying climax early Sunday morning October 17, 1993. Caroline Witt and her new boyfriend, Brian Weiwede, happened to see Wendt at a gas station. Following a hostile exchange of words, the men scuffled. Caroline Witt and her boyfriend drove off, but Wendt swiftly pursued them, bumping their car before driving on. Wendt then made a U-turn and sped back to crash head-on into their vehicle. The impact of the collision killed Caroline Witt. As her mother recalls, "The next time I saw Caroline she was under Kristoffer Wendt's car."[14]

These women, and thousands of others like them, were victims of stalking. Although stalking has been referred to as the "crime of the '90s," such behavior is hardly new. As noted by Lieutenant John Lane of the Los Angeles Police Department, "These behaviors have existed in our society for a long time, but we're just now starting to put a label on them."[15]

Stalking is frequently defined as "the willful, malicious, and repeated following or harassing of another person." The victims include individuals presently at risk of physical or emotional harm, as well as those who are being followed or harassed, but are not in imminent danger.

Stalking is considerably more widespread than most people believe. Anyone can be stalked—victims of this crime include men, women, and children. Although celebrity stalkings are frequently highlighted in the media, the vast majority of stalking victims are everyday people. For the most part, they tend to be women. Experts predict that at some point in their lives one out of every twenty American women will be stalked.[16] Often their stalkers prove to be people they once loved or shared their lives with. Seventy-five to eighty percent of stalking incidents involve individuals who were either formerly married or dating. In 1992, 1,500 women were stalked and murdered by former husbands or boyfriends.[17]

Even those who survive being stalked frequently find that the crime devastates their lives. This may be partly because it's frequently difficult to know what the stalker will do next or how far he or she may ultimately go. There isn't a predictable stalking pattern. The threats and harassment may last for days or weeks or continue for years. In some instances, the stalker limits the harassment to annoying phone calls and letters while in other cases the destructive behavior escalates to assault or homicide.

Living in fear, stalked individuals often hesitate to answer the phone, go to and from school or work alone, or attend social or cultural events as they had in

An obsessed stalker may follow the victim's every move.

the past. At times these victims may be forced to disguise their identity and move to another state, leaving their family and friends behind. They may also suffer from a broad range of physical or emotional ailments resulting from the ongoing stress.

Yet despite the potentially grievous consequences, society tends to minimize stalking's effect on its victims. Initially, victims may be told that the stalker seems harmless or even that they should feel complimented by all the attention. In many cases, authorities do not take stalking seriously until it takes a sinister turn, resulting in injury or damage to the victim's person or property.

This book is about stalking. It charts our growing awareness of the crime while exploring such areas as the connection between stalking and domestic violence, antistalking legislation, and what victims can do to protect themselves. It offers an important view of an often underestimated, but potentially disastrous, crime.

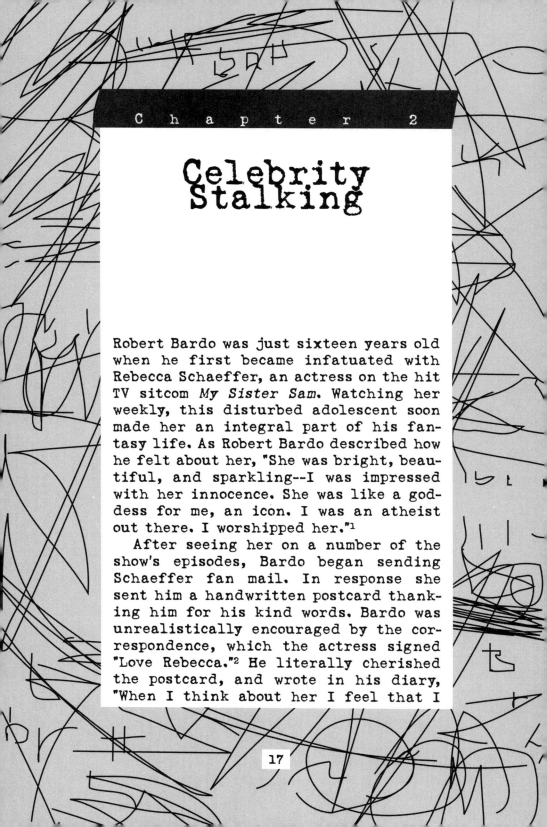

Celebrity Stalking

Robert Bardo was just sixteen years old
when he first became infatuated with
Rebecca Schaeffer, an actress on the hit
TV sitcom *My Sister Sam*. Watching her
weekly, this disturbed adolescent soon
made her an integral part of his fantasy life. As Robert Bardo described how
he felt about her, "She was bright, beau-
tiful, and sparkling--I was impressed
with her innocence. She was like a god-
dess for me, an icon. I was an atheist
out there. I worshipped her."[1]

　　After seeing her on a number of the
show's episodes, Bardo began sending
Schaeffer fan mail. In response she
sent him a handwritten postcard thank-
ing him for his kind words. Bardo was
unrealistically encouraged by the correspondence, which the actress signed
"Love Rebecca."[2] He literally cherished
the postcard, and wrote in his diary,
"When I think about her I feel that I

want to become famous and impress her."[3] Yet on the same page Bardo left this chillingly foreboding comment, "How do I know if the table and paper before me is just a field of electronic impulses. How can I be sure if this is reality?"[4]

Bardo was clearly out of touch with reality and filled with unrealistic expectations when he left his Arizona home in June 1987 and traveled to California to be with the star. Carrying a large teddy bear and a letter for her, he arrived at the studio where the TV sitcom was filmed. Security personnel denied him entrance. He left, but because Bardo believed that Schaeffer was "turning arrogant," he returned the following month with a knife. Nevertheless, when he was again turned away, he just headed home.

Robert Bardo appeared less preoccupied with Schaeffer in 1988 as his interest in pop music stars Debbie Gibson and Tiffany grew. But his fixation on Schaeffer resumed in 1989 after she appeared in a sexually explicit scene in the film *Scenes from the Class Struggle in Beverly Hills*. Robert Bardo was enraged over her role in the movie. He felt the sweet, innocent starlet had turned into just "another Hollywood whore."[5]

After reading how a stalker had gotten the address of an actress he nearly stabbed to death, Bardo paid a private detective $250.00 to find out where Schaeffer lived. In Arizona he had to be twenty-one to purchase a firearm, so Bardo persuaded his older brother to buy a gun for him. He put the weapon, along with hollow-point bullets (which explode on impact) and a lengthy letter to Schaeffer, in a plastic bag before boarding an overnight bus to California.

Bardo wandered through Schaeffer's neighborhood for about an hour and a half before going to her apartment. He rang the buzzer, waited until Rebecca Schaeffer came to the door, and handed her the letter he had written. Thinking he was a messenger, Schaeffer thanked Bardo and told him to "take care" before she closed the thick glass security door and returned to her apartment. This, however, wasn't the last time she would see Robert Bardo that day. He returned to her apartment complex about an hour later and this time shot her in the chest when she came to the door. Schaeffer died as Bardo fled the crime scene. He was later tried for the actress's murder, and in December 1991, he was sentenced to life in prison without parole.

Celebrities are often ideal targets for stalkers. Performing on TV or in films, these individuals are frequently highly visible to millions of people. Psychiatrist Park Dietz, an acknowledged expert on stalking, notes that a substantial number of Hollywood personalities have been the recipients of "strange unwanted attention" from fans.[6] Celebrity stalking has even become something of a trend. A 1989 National Institute of Justice report indicates that in the past twenty-five years alone, there have been as many attacks on celebrities by people with mental disorders as had occurred in the previous one hundred and seventy-five years.

Fan clubs, movie magazines, and television talk shows allow fans some degree of access to their media idols. Yet there are individuals who go beyond the appropriate boundaries, creating a rich fantasy life around a celebrity. One common delusion is that they actually know the celebrity and are an important part of their idol's life. This was certainly true of Rebecca Schaeffer's murderer, Robert Bardo. During an interview while in prison, Bardo explained, "It happens 'cause they're in the limelight. . . . She was very open with her personality. . . . When I read those magazine articles, I feel like I know them [the stars]. . . . It's like they've been with you their whole life. . . . To me, my victim wasn't a stranger."[7]

Charles Russell Gilberg, who stalked popular singing star Whitney Houston, felt similarly. When charged by police, Gilberg claimed he had a love affair with Houston and that they had a son named after him whom they called "little Charlie." At the same time, Gilberg asserted that he was the father of Whitney Houston's husband, Bobbi Brown.

In court, Gilberg said he was innocent and had never stalked Houston. He further indicated that the pop star's mother, Cissy Houston, was persecuting him, and he feared the Houston family might falsely accuse him of violating the court-imposed restraining order. Houston's attorney, Thomas Weisenbeck, asked that the court order a psychiatric exam for Gilberg after learning that the stalker had previously been involved in violent incidents in both New Jersey and Michigan, including threatening his roommate with a butcher knife. He had also been disciplined while in the Marine Corps in connection with a 1977 assault. The Houston family grew especially concerned once it was disclosed that Gilberg had tried to buy two guns in a Michigan gun shop. "The store had revoked those sales, but we would like to know if he has acquired other firearms," their attorney stated.[8]

Late night talk show host David Letterman was also stalked by an individual who believed she was intimately involved with him. As early as 1988, Margaret Ray insisted that she was really Letterman's wife. Within the next five years, she was arrested eight

Robert Bardo listens in court after his arrest for the murder of actress Rebecca Schaeffer.

times for an assortment of trespassing violations. On various occasions when Letterman wasn't at his Connecticut home, Ray broke into his house with her young son and drove his car around town.

Another celebrity, Michael J. Fox, was hounded by a persistent young woman named Tina Marie Ledbetter, who referred to herself as Fox's "Number One Fan." Ledbetter both admired his work and believed she was in love with the actor. Following Fox's marriage to actress Tracey Pollen, he began receiving letters from Ledbetter. She wrote to Fox 6,200 times in under a year, and her messages often seemed more menacing than admiring. She once wrote that if Fox didn't immediately divorce Pollen he would die.

Being stalked can be especially disconcerting to celebrities as they frequently feel they are too visible to hide. In surveying the situation, stalking authority Gavin de Becker amassed more than three hundred thousand unusual letters and presents sent to celebrities by fans who had crossed the line of acceptable behavior. Among these were a sample tube of tooth paste, a pencil, a half-eaten candy bar, snips of human hair, a thousand-page letter, animal feces, and photos of corpses with the star's face pasted over them.

Celebrities such as Whitney Houston are frequently targeted by stalkers. Their lives in the limelight can make it impossible to hide.

While receiving such items from a seemingly disturbed fan can be stressful, studies show that there is no sure way to predict if a stalker will become violent. Researchers note that a stalker's spoken or written threat is not a clear indication of whether the celebrity is in danger or will even ever be approached. However, celebrity stalking experts stress that a public personality is more likely to be approached by a stalker if several of the following conditions exist:

- Through his or her letter, the stalker expresses a desire to approach the celebrity;
- The stalker mentions "sharing a special destiny or fate" with the celebrity;
- The stalker cites a specific date, time, or place where "something would happen to the celebrity";
- The stalker writes over ten letters to a celebrity;
- The stalker mentions a weapon in his or her letters;
- The stalker continues writing to the celebrity from more than one place of residence;
- Although there may be gaps of weeks or months in his or her correspondence, the stalker writes to the same celebrity for over a year; and
- Besides writing to the celebrity, the stalker attempts to telephone that person either at his or her home or workplace.

Television, film, and rock stars aren't the only visible figures likely to be stalked. Senators, congresspersons, and U.S. Supreme Court judges are also fairly common targets. Researchers believe that public officials are frequently stalked because they "must take public positions on such charged issues as abortion, gun control, capital punishment, gay rights, . . . and military spending."[9]

As do film and TV stars, public officials often

receive a broad array of inappropriate objects in the mail. These have included blood and semen samples, nude photographs of a stalker, as well as copies of a stalker's birth certificate or passport. The demands and claims made by stalkers to public officials may be comparably outrageous. One demanded that the president of the United States be immediately impeached and arrested, while another claimed to have become so enraged as she wrote her letter that she stabbed herself in the eye.

One highly publicized stalking incident involving an elected official and his family was that of U.S. Senator Bob Krueger. In 1983, Texas rancher and businessman Bob Krueger decided to run for the U.S. Senate. Early in his campaign, Krueger hired airplane pilot Thomas Michael Humphrey to fly him and his family throughout the state for personal appearances. Humphrey, who had a small single-engine plane, performed his duties adequately and was generally well thought of by the Kruegers and their campaign staff. When Bob Krueger lost the Democratic primary by a slim margin in May 1984, however, the pilot seemed more upset than the candidate. Explaining that the Kruegers had come to mean a great deal to him, Humphrey appeared unable to move on. The pilot soon made a habit of frequently dropping by to visit with them. At first Bob Krueger would talk to him at length, trying to cheer up his former employee. But after a while he took a more direct approach, telling Humphrey, "Tom, you need to get on with your life. We're getting on with ours and we need you to respect our privacy the same way we'll respect yours."[10]

At this point, Thomas Michael Humphrey's behavior turned increasingly obsessive and bizarre. At first he called the Krueger household about a dozen times a day, but the number soon grew to as many as 120 daily calls. His harassment of the

Kruegers intensified as he frequently left unnerving notes in their mailbox and on their front door.

Bob Krueger's wife, Kathleen, remembers the fear she felt when Humphrey unexpectedly arrived at her front door one day while she was home alone. She recalls:

> Tom rang the doorbell, and I opened the door. He stepped inside and reached forward to give me a hug. His grip tightened and I realized he might not let go. It wasn't sexual, but it was eerie. I knew something wasn't right. . . . So I said, "Tom, would you go out with me to check the mail?" We went outside, and I knew it was too early for the mail but I was able to say good bye to him on the street.[11]

This was the last time Kathleen Krueger ever let him into her home, although some days he would stand at the front door ringing the bell for twenty minutes. Humphrey also invaded the Krueger's privacy in other ways. He even rented a house across the street from theirs and watched them from behind his curtains.

Initially the Kruegers tried to reason with Humphrey, but nothing they said could end his obsession with them. They were somewhat relieved after hearing that he had moved to California, but Humphrey continued to call the Texas couple from there. Sometimes he would ask for money; on other occasions he didn't speak at all. After a while the Kruegers would just hang up on his calls. They also turned to law enforcement authorities for help but were told by local police, a county attorney, and the FBI that nothing could be done until Humphrey tried to physically harm them.

Thomas Michael Humphrey's harassment of them continued for several years. When the couple got an unlisted phone number, he would fill the answering machine at Bob Krueger's office with threatening messages. At Christmastime in 1987, he left the following gruesome threat for Bob Krueger:

> I'm going to kill you. I'm going to kill you. I'm going to kill you. I've hired a . . . killer to put a .22-caliber to your head while you lie sleeping next to your wife. You won't be much of an ambassador [Bob Krueger had been ambassador-at-large to Mexico] with a hole in your head.[12]

Because Humphrey made a specific death threat and the phone call came from across state lines, the FBI could finally intervene. Humphrey was charged with extortion and making death threats, and after pleading guilty in May 1989, he was sentenced to twelve months in prison.

The Kruegers' relief was short-lived. Following Humphrey's release, the harassment again intensified. "Tom's threats often seemed to jibe with family holidays or important occasions," Kathleen Krueger explains. "I can remember one Christmas Eve when I was preparing a meal for Bob's relatives. I was standing at the stove trying to stir a pot of food and just sobbing because I was so afraid. His threats had become more gruesome when I was pregnant."[13]

Thomas Michael Humphrey was arrested and imprisoned again in 1990. When he continued to engage in similar behavior after his release, he was arrested a third time. Through the years, Humphrey's stalking had caused the Kruegers considerable emotional distress. As Kathleen Krueger testified before the Senate Judiciary Committee in 1993:

> Most of all I am afraid to be alone—alone in my home, whether it be day or night. Alone with our children, whether it be in our backyard or walking the New Braunfels square. Bob has always done a lot of traveling for his work and . . . we try to make sure someone is with me day and night. We've shared our home with someone each

year—this year, with a full-time college student who comes home at night and on weekends. . . . Recently Bob and I had lunch with the U.S. attorney assigned to our case. The attorney said something I will never forget. He said, "In all my years of law enforcement, I have only two or three times stood next to a defendant and thought—this is a killer. In every case I have come to find out that yes that person had killed someone or, soon after did kill someone." Then he paused and said, "I don't have a good feeling about Tom Humphrey."[14]

With numerous sports receiving wide media coverage in recent years, athletes have also been increasingly stalked. This has been especially true for women. Only a generation ago, threats of violence against them wasn't a serious problem as so few females were involved in sports. But with significantly more women in both the college and professional sports arena, these athletes now draw a sizable amount of monetary winnings and product endorsement contracts. Unfortunately, the negative side of the limelight is that they have also attracted more unwanted and sometimes sinister attention.

German figure skating star Katarina Witt was pursued for months by a man who set out from California

The rise in popularity of women's sporting events has resulted in an increase of stalking cases involving women athletes. Katarina Witt, shown here in 1985, experienced this unfortunate by-product of fame and success firsthand.

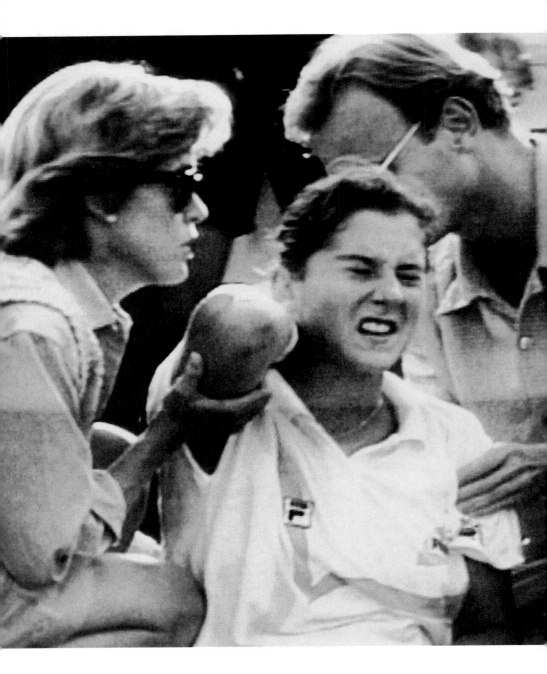

to find the skater's home in Altendorf, Germany. The stalker had also sent Witt some disturbing notes and gifts, including a nude photograph of himself along with various inappropriately worded marriage proposals. Although Witt repeatedly asked him to leave her alone, the stalker persisted. He was finally apprehended by the FBI after writing Witt a letter containing the threatening passage, "Please don't be afraid when God allows me to take you out of your body and hold you tight! Then you'll know there is life beyond the flesh."[15]

Tennis champion Monica Seles was stalked by a man who eventually tried to kill her. Gunter Parche, the stalker, had closely followed Seles throughout a week-long 1993 tennis tournament in Hamburg, Germany. Without warning, while Seles was seated during a break in an April 30 tennis match, he thrust a nine-inch, jagged-edged boning knife into her back.

Ironically, thirty-eight-year-old Parche hadn't been obsessed with Seles but was in love with her German tennis rival Steffi Graff. Although he'd never met Graff, Parche had erected a shrine to her in his home consisting of tennis videos and posters featuring Graff. Through his attack on Seles, Parche hoped to enhance Graff's career opportunities by eliminating the competition. Although Seles survived the stabbing, she suffered sufficient physical and emotional injuries to keep her out of professional tennis for two years.

Sadly, when tried for his crime in a German court of law, Gunter Parche was given a two-year suspended

Tennis star Monica Seles after being stabbed by Gunter Parche.

31

sentence and set free. Outraged at the leniency shown her assailant, Seles said, "He gets to go back to his life, but I can't because I'm still recovering from this attack."[16]

Are female athletes more likely to be stalked than their male counterparts because they are presumed to be more vulnerable? Although these women may be muscular and well toned, a 5' 2" figure skater weighing 105 pounds is not likely to do as well in physical confrontation as a male football linebacker. University of Indiana social psychologist Edward Hirt offers some insight into the phenomenon: "Women athletes are an interesting mix of perceptions. Do you view them as athletes in the same context as males? Or do you view them as women in terms of their femininity? That doesn't happen with men."[17]

It's been further suggested that the rise in stalking affecting female athletes may be related to a backlash against feminism and the recent career advances achieved by women. The money, trophies, and fame presently enjoyed by many women athletes were once exclusively reserved for men. "The woman athlete represents a symbol of frustration and a feeling of displacement that many men feel," suggests Northwestern University Law professor Jane Larson. "Many men have lost control over their work and their own lives."[18]

Successful sportswomen generally have an abundance of mental strength and fortitude. Such qualities, which are undoubtedly instrumental in becoming a world-class athlete, have also helped women cope with the stress stalking generates. Yet while these women may survive, they frequently pay a high price for fame and glory. As Lenore Lawton, spokeswoman for the Woman's Sports Foundation, summarizes, "Now, you are not only being judged by

In some cases, stalked individuals have
hired bodyguards to protect them.

your performance, but you also have to fear for your life."[19]

It's a price paid by any person who succeeds in the eyes of the world. Towards the end of her life, former First Lady Jacqueline Kennedy Onassis was stalked by a man who was eventually arrested with a .44-caliber handgun and a pack of hollow-point bullets on his person. Comedian and film star Jerry Lewis's stalker had repeatedly shown up at both the celebrity's home and office claiming to have a gun. A stalker who said he was pop star Madonna's husband scaled an eight-foot gate surrounding her California estate attempting to reach her.

Incidents such as these have prompted a growing number of celebrities to secure private, around-the-clock security. According to California State University media psychologist Stuart Fischoff, "For everyone who is going to become a celebrity today, there is an unwritten contract. The minute you put yourself in the spotlight, you become a target for the weirdos of society."[20]

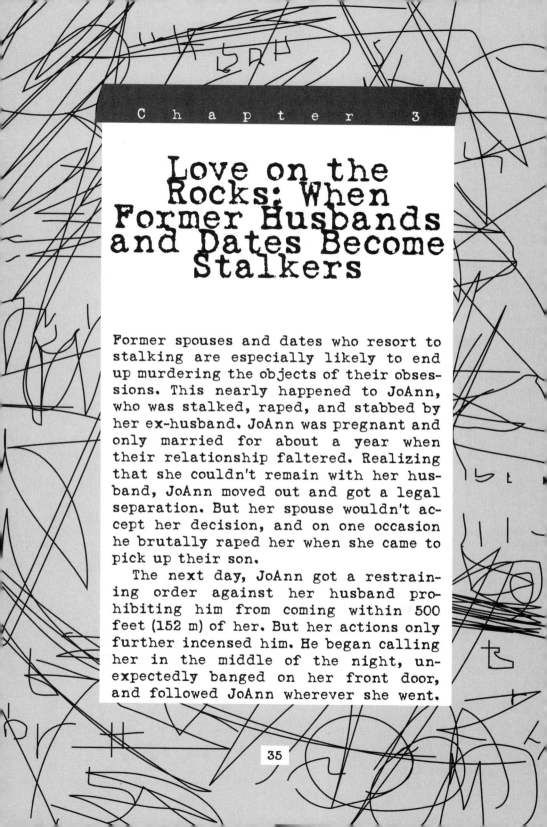

Love on the Rocks: When Former Husbands and Dates Become Stalkers

Former spouses and dates who resort to stalking are especially likely to end up murdering the objects of their obsessions. This nearly happened to JoAnn, who was stalked, raped, and stabbed by her ex-husband. JoAnn was pregnant and only married for about a year when their relationship faltered. Realizing that she couldn't remain with her husband, JoAnn moved out and got a legal separation. But her spouse wouldn't accept her decision, and on one occasion he brutally raped her when she came to pick up their son.

The next day, JoAnn got a restraining order against her husband prohibiting him from coming within 500 feet (152 m) of her. But her actions only further incensed him. He began calling her in the middle of the night, unexpectedly banged on her front door, and followed JoAnn wherever she went.

JoAnn recalls his unnerving obsession with her:

> I would get in my car and he would be standing right there in front of me. So, I started having to look behind me, wondering if he was outside my door in the middle of the night. He broke into my car a couple of times . . . just moving things around and making me wonder, where is he? When is he going to be here? What is he going to do next?[1]

To her dismay, JoAnn didn't have to wait very long to find out. One day, JoAnn's husband jumped her as she sat in her car and began stabbing her with a Philips head screwdriver. JoAnn screamed, but when nobody heard her cries, she used her knee to press the car horn. She remembers:

> People start coming around, and they're like, banging on the door, 'Get him off her! Get him off her!' and so he says 'If you don't stay away, I'm going to kill her right now!' . . . And he stabbed me, eleven times he stabbed me, all in my ear, this side of my neck, and down my arm.[2]

When her husband finally tried to flee, four men in the crowd chased and caught him. He later pleaded guilty to attempted murder, aggravated assault, and kidnapping. JoAnn was lucky to have survived—after examining her wounds her doctor told her that she had come within a centimeter of being killed.

Another frightening case involved a young woman named Kimberly who was stalked by her ex-boyfriend. Enraged over her departure, he scratched the word "bitch" on her car, put sugar in the vehicle's gas tank, and cut the tires. He also threatened to kill Kimberly and tampered with her door locks to let her know that he could always get to her. Although he was

In some cases, stalkers have hidden in their victims' cars.

arrested and is currently in jail, law enforcement personnel have warned Kimberly that she may not be no-
tified when he is released.

Meanwhile, Kimberly lives in a continual state of
terror. She describes her feelings, saying, "I don't
know. I'm still paranoid when I hear people walking
through the halls. I don't know if he got out or whatever. I'm afraid to go to my garage. I'm afraid to go
wash my clothes. I haven't been going to work. My job
is threatening to fire me. I don't know . . . I'm afraid to
leave the house."[3]

Although most former spouses or dates who turn
to stalking are male, women sometimes engage in this
behavior too. Among the most well known of these
cases is that of Betty Broderick, who fatally shot her
ex-husband and his new wife as they slept in their
bed. Broderick deeply resented her husband leaving
her for a woman who some said seemed like a
younger version of herself. Consumed with jealousy
and rage, the first Mrs. Broderick hounded the couple
incessantly. Frequently she left obscene messages on
their telephone answering machine and vandalized
their home. Following the murders, Broderick said that
she hadn't planned to harm the pair, but had felt like
dying herself. Yet rather than attempting suicide, she
committed the double murder.

Frequently, individuals who can't let go are involved in obsessive relationships. Unlike people in

Though the majority of stalking cases
involve men stalking women, the reverse
does occur. In some cases, the stalker and
victim are of the same sex.

39

healthy relationships, these individuals experience a desperate need to cling to the person rejecting them. "Obsessive lovers truly believe—sometimes without realizing it—that their 'One Magic Person' alone can make them feel happy and fulfilled, solve all their problems, give them the passion they've yearned for, and make them feel more wanted and loved than they've ever felt before," notes psychotherapist and author Dr. Susan Forward. "With all this power, the One Magic Person becomes more than a lover—he or she becomes a necessity of life."[4]

Although various cases differ, researchers have identified the following personality traits among spouses or dating partners who resort to stalking:

- Low self-esteem;
- Feelings of dependency;
- Tendencies to view people as possessions;
- Fears of abandonment;
- Feelings of severe jealousy;
- Irritability;
- Alcohol problems (in 40 percent).[5]

Bob, who's tried to stop stalking women who reject him, has exhibited a number of these characteristics. He describes what it's been like this way:

> Once you're rejected completely, and you can't find any way out, the symptoms start persisting, and you feel bad. . . . I remember going to a girl-friend's house, banging on the door in the middle of the night, ultimately winding up smashing windows and screaming. And there were several instances like that. The repeated phone calls. The badgering at work. The notes left on cars. And these are just minor examples. Major

examples would be . . . going to a bar where my girlfriend was hanging out and drinking and carousing with fellows, or putting a couple of nails in her tires, figuring, "This will really fix her wagon. This will alleviate some of how bad I feel."[6]

Margaret, a thirty-four-year-old paralegal, has felt and acted similarly to Bob. Recalling how she stalked a former boyfriend who rejected her, she regretfully notes, "I can't believe I did all those things. The phone calls, the drive-bys, the letters, the tantrums, the threats . . . it just wasn't me. But it took me so long to get him out of my head. The way he looked, the way he smelled, the way he touched me . . . he drove me crazy."[7]

Dr. Suzette Rush, who counsels people like Margaret and Bob, notes that former spouses or dating partners who become stalkers often place their victims and themselves in potentially explosive situations. She explains:

I think that one of the core issues is that these are men (or women) who do not have very good relationships with people (and) are very easily prone to feeling abandoned. . . . And that's part of the reason why . . . they've got to keep that person. . . . They're very needy. . . . And . . . that fear of that person leaving them is just so scary and so overwhelming for them that they'll do anything to control that person.[8]

While stalkers generally tend to be unpredictable, former spouses or dates who engage in this behavior sometimes follow a particular pattern that intensifies with time. Wendy Collier of Victim Protective Services in Colorado outlines and describes the three general phases of this cycle.

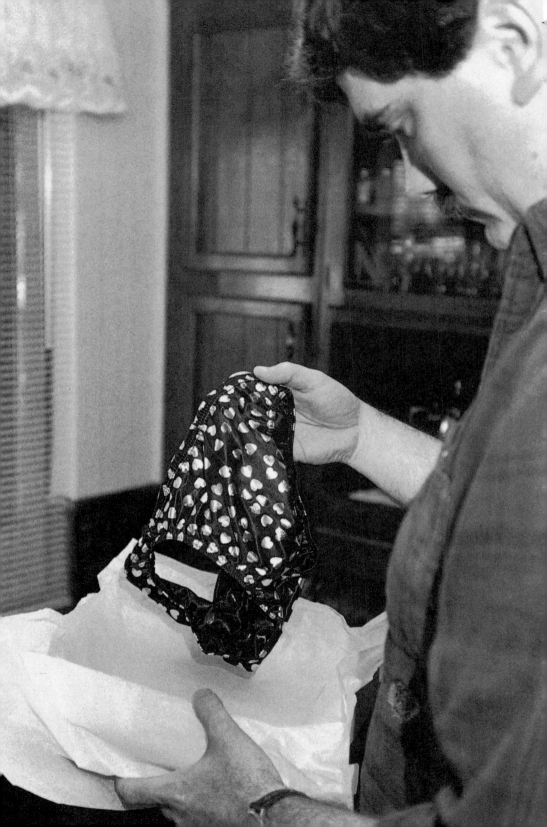

Phase 1
The Tension Building Phase

In this initial phase, the stalker usually begins with relatively minor intrusions into the victim's privacy. These may include making repeated telephone calls and sending inappropriate letters and gifts. When the stalker doesn't achieve his or her goal, the negative behavior escalates. Attempting to intimidate the victim, the stalker may threaten and follow that person as well as vandalize his or her property.

Phase 2
The Explosive or Acutely Violent Phase

Here a stalker's low-level aggressive acts snowball into full-scale violence. At this point the offender may resort to physical assault, rape, and kidnapping. In some cases this extreme abuse may continue for hours or even days. In the worst instances the stalking trauma ends with the victim's murder.

Phase 3
The Hearts and Flowers Phase

The hearts and flowers phase occurs in some, though not all, stalking incidents that follow this pattern. When present, this phase usually takes place between phase 1 and phase 2 and can take any of several different forms.

Many stalking victims receive inappropriate, unwanted gifts from their pursuers.

43

In the hearts and flowers phase, stalkers will often apologetically present flowers to their victims. After a while, however, the threatening behavior usually resumes.

The stalker may become intensely contrite and apologetic for his or her hostile attitude and past deeds. He may send his victim candy and flowers and promise that things will be different in the future. During this period, also referred to as "the honeymoon stage," stalkers often beg their victims for forgiveness.

In other cases, the stalker may merely stop harassing his or her victim, allowing the person to mistakenly believe that the nightmare is finally over. At times, individuals who abandon security precautions during this phase are caught off guard when their stalkers resume the harassment.

In still other situations, the stalker actually switches victims during the hearts and flowers phase. As Wendy Collier explains, "[Some stalkers] abandon their current victim and redirect their fixation to more challenging and vulnerable prey—someone who is not yet alert to their dangerous patterns and treachery."[9]

It is important to remember that although the cycle described here is characteristic of many former spouses and dating partners who become stalkers, it isn't true for everyone. In some instances the violence never escalates, while other times the stalker turns dangerously aggressive almost immediately. Therefore, it is crucial that anyone being stalked remain acutely aware of both the circumstances and nuances of his or her case. For some, it could mean the difference between life and death.

Young Stalkers--
Young Victims

Stalking! The subject evokes images of
adults involved in dangerously obsessive entanglements. Yet it has become
increasingly clear that this crime is
not limited to those over twenty-one. Unfortunately, there are teenage stalkers
and sometimes even younger victims.

Sixteen-year-old Lynn (name changed)
learned this firsthand when her ex-
boyfriend began stalking her following
their breakup. He started by continually parking near her house and looking into her windows. Then came the
phone calls--sometimes he would threaten
to kill her, other times he would comment on some aspect of her appearance or
behavior to assure Lynn that he knew
her every move. Lynn recalls, "I'd go inside and change after school, and he'd
make a call saying, 'Oh well, I liked
your hair better up (or down, however I

had it)' . . . [or] 'I liked the sweater you were wearing better before.'"[1]

Besides watching her home, Lynn's stalker constantly followed her. He trailed the young woman both on foot and in his car, and whether she went shopping or on a date, he would call later to discuss the outing with her. As a result, Lynn felt that her former boyfriend could harm her whenever he wished and that she wasn't safe anywhere.

"I never know what's going to happen," she explains. "I don't feel safe taking out the dogs even. I cannot walk up to a little store down the street because I'm afraid he's going to approach me, and I'm not sure what might happen. I walk around constantly scared with a little can of mace . . . knowing that that's the only protection I have against him."[2]

Lynn got a restraining order against her former boyfriend but nothing changed. The stalker was always gone by the time the police arrived. Ultimately, Lynn's family had to drastically alter their lifestyle to protect their daughter. "This is one of the most frightening things we've ever had to deal with," her mother explains. "We've had to change our whole way of living. The curtains are [drawn] tight . . . and when we leave the house, we have to watch every single time. The prosecutors and the police have told us, very definitely, you watch when you leave the house, when you come back and when you get in and out of your car, and . . . [Lynn can't be left] alone."[3]

While it is distressing to have a family member stalked, it can also be traumatic to find that someone in your family is a stalker. That's exactly what Jody (name changed) had to deal with when she learned that her teenage brother had been stalking a girl for more than four years. At first Jody had been too young to realize what was going on. "He would go out every night in black or camouflage," she remembers. "He would just say he was going out to play war games with his friends, or whatever, and it was a couple of years before I even found out what he was doing."[4]

Each evening, her brother went to a wooded area surrounding the home of a young girl he was stalking. If the girl was in her bedroom on the second floor, he would climb a tree and watch her from there. If she went to her gym downstairs, he would hide in the bushes surrounding the house to look through the lower windows.

At times he would call the girl, utter obscenities, and hang up. He would also occasionally bring some of his friends into the woods with him to watch her. Although the victim and her family felt they knew who the stalker was, the police needed proof to intervene. When the victim called Jody to ask for help, she could only advise her on what she thought her brother might be thinking or what his next move might be. The stalking ended when Jody's brother finally left home and moved away. Jody doesn't know his present whereabouts but has learned that he is wanted for rape in at least two counties.

Anyone who thinks teenage stalking isn't as potentially lethal as the adult version is wrong—dead wrong. This was inescapably evident after seventeen-year-old Mindy was brutally murdered in July 1994 by a former boyfriend who had been stalking her.

Mindy, who had dated her murderer since she was fifteen, had originally planned to marry him when they were older. But as time passed she became

---

A stalker may try to enter a victim's home forcefully.

aware of his violent nature and left him. Her enraged boyfriend retaliated by stalking her. He began by leaving Mindy letters and following her. Also, her family suspected that on several occasions he had broken into their home, taking some of Mindy's possessions.

One evening, however, he unexpectedly called Mindy and politely told her that he was finally willing to accept their breakup. Claiming that now he only wished her happiness, he asked that she stop by the following day to pick up the items he had taken from her home. Her mother warned her not to go, preferring to let him keep everything, but Mindy went anyway. As she drove up his driveway, he shot her to death.

Psychologist Barry Lubetkin attributes some of the potential danger in teenage stalking to the stalker's possessiveness and the victim's naiveté in selecting an appropriate romantic interest. "We have something called teenage territorialism where teenagers become extremely possessive of that which they believe belongs to them," suggests Lubetkin. "One of the great problems with boys is that when you say no to a boy, he hears maybe very often. . . . Sometimes it's his problem and it has nothing to do with the girl . . . but boys don't hear no. The other thing that teenagers must be aware of is how to screen the new relationship. . . . Ask him about his old girlfriend. How jealous does he get? Has he been violent in the past? We spend more time looking for a new car than we do screening new relationships and teenagers are particularly naive about this."[5]

Unfortunately, some stalking victims have been very young children. Crystal Peterson of Independence, Oregon, was just seven years old when she noticed a man staring at her from the street as she splashed in the swimming pool on her lawn. Feeling uncomfortable under his steady gaze, Crystal held her breath and ducked under the water to hide. When the child came up for air, the man was gone and Crystal thought no more about it.

She had no way of knowing that the man she had seen that day had rented a room in the house across the street and had become obsessed with her. During the next three years, he would secretly watch her from his window for hours, and by May 1991, he began taking steps to interact with Crystal. He would leave unsigned adoring letters for the girl on her doorstep. Seeing the poor spelling and juvenile handwriting, the Petersons thought the flattering notes were merely from a boy Crystal's age.

But before long, the stalker's correspondence took on a darker tone. Now the letters often contained the jealous ranting of an obviously older man who didn't hesitate to use foul language. Crystal's parents realized that the letter writer apparently knew their daughter's daily activities; he probably lived nearby.

To safeguard Crystal, the Petersons kept their blinds drawn and sometimes even hesitated to let their children play outdoors. One of Crystal's parents walked her to school every day while school authorities also kept a close watch on the girl. All these precautions stripped away the spontaneity that had formerly characterized Crystal's existence. "I have to stay where they can see me during recess," the child complained. "If my friends want to play somewhere else, I'm left there all alone."[6]

Nights were especially difficult for the Petersons. As Crystal's father worked evenings, all the children felt safer sleeping near their mother. The younger ones slept in her bed while the older offspring remained on blankets on the floor. Both Crystal and her mother kept fireplace pokers at their sides. Because the stalker always delivered his letters after dark, they feared that one night he might try to break in.

On October 27, 1991, while the Petersons were away, the stalker did enter their home. There he came across Crystal's grandmother's phone number, which he decided to dial at three o'clock in the morning. Sounding as though he were either drunk or drugged, he told her grandmother that if he couldn't have Crystal, no one would. Before hanging up, he mentioned that one day he and Crystal would be together in heaven.

Trying to trap him, Crystal's mother left the stalker a note suggesting that they meet. He agreed, but prior to the meeting he left another letter revealing his address. This enabled the police to finally arrest twenty-four-year-old Robert Thomas Coker. When apprehended, he had still other letters to Crystal with him.

Another frightening instance in which a young girl was stalked occurred in 1993 in New York. A fifty-six-year-old tennis coach named Gary Wilensky was discharged by the mother of a young tennis student after she became suspicious of the coach's intense interest in her daughter. But Wilensky was obsessed with the girl and refused to stay away. He later tried to kidnap both his former student and her mother after the child played in an upstate New York tennis championship, but they managed to get away.

Police investigating the crime soon uncovered a chamber of horrors that the tennis coach had designed for his young victim. He had rented a nearby cabin and stocked it with handcuffs and chains. Wilensky's New York City apartment also contained an assortment of pornographic videos featuring young people being stalked and sexually abused. Just as he was about to be arrested, Wilensky committed suicide. It was revealed afterwards that he had stalked children for years.

Very young children may be particularly vulnerable to stalkers, not realizing that a stranger who repeatedly approaches them in a friendly manner over a period of time may still be potentially dangerous. The warning—don't talk to strangers—may not seem applicable to someone the child thinks he already knows.

Stalking
and the Law

Until the early 1990s, victims had little
legal recourse in dealing with stalkers. Prior to the passage of antistalking legislation, some states required
that victims wait until the stalker either broke into their home or physically
assaulted them before law enforcement
authorities could act.

This was largely because the main in-
strument of protection available to
those being stalked was a restraining
order (also known as an order of protection) requiring the stalker to remain a
predetermined distance from the targeted person. But these court orders are
frequently ineffective for two reasons.
Jurisdictional boundaries often limit
their enforcement, but even more impor-
tantly, perpetrators can only be penal-
ized after they have violated the order
and have perhaps seriously harmed
or even killed their victim. At times,

ATTORNEY OR PARTY WITHOUT ATTORNEY (Name and Address):	TELEPHONE NO	FOR COURT USE ONLY
		FILED

ATTORNEY FOR (Name): IN PRO PER

SUPERIOR COURT OF CALIFORNIA, COUNTY OF
STREET ADDRESS
MAILING ADDRESS
CITY AND ZIP CODE
BRANCH NAME

PERSON TO BE PROTECTED:

PERSON TO BE RESTRAINED:

☐ PETITIONER/PLAINTIFF	
☐ RESPONDENT/DEFENDANT	
☐ PETITIONER/PLAINTIFF	
☐ RESPONDENT/DEFENDANT	

RESTRAINING ORDER AFTER HEARING (CLETS)
(Domestic Violence Prevention)

CASE NUMBER

This form may be used in conjunction with the Findings and Order After Hearing form (rule 1296.31) if the court makes additional orders.

1. This proceeding was heard
   on (date): FEB 28 1995   at (time): 11:00   in Dept.: 12   Room:
   by judge (name):   ☐ Temporary Judge

2. a. ☑ Petitioner/plaintiff and respondent/defendant were personally present at the court hearing. No additional proof of service of these restraining orders is required.
   b. ☐ Petitioner/plaintiff was personally present and proof of service of the Order to Show Cause was provided.

THE COURT FINDS

3. a. The restrained person is (name):

   Sex: ☑ M   ☐ F   Ht 5'7"   Wt. 140   Hair Color: B   Eye Color: BI   Race: W   Age 30   Date of birth:

   b. The protected person is (name):

   c. The protected family and household members are (names):

THE COURT ORDERS

THIS ORDER, EXCEPT FOR ANY AWARD OF CHILD CUSTODY OR VISITATION, SHALL EXPIRE AT MIDNIGHT ON
(date):   FEB 28 1996

4. The restrained person
   a. shall not contact, molest, attack, strike, threaten, sexually assault, batter, telephone, or otherwise disturb the peace of the protected person ☑ and family or household members.
   b. ☑ shall stay at least 100 yards away from the protected persons and
      (1) ☑ protected person's residence
      (2) ☑ protected person's workplace
      (3) ☑ protected person's children's school or child care
      (4) ☐ other (specify):

      ☑ except as provided in item 5b (visitation).
   c. ☑ shall immediately move from (address):
      and take only personal clothing and effects.

- *Taking or concealing a child in violation of this order may be a felony and punishable by confinement in state prison, a fine, or both.*
- *Any person subject to a restraining order is prohibited from obtaining or purchasing or attempting to purchase a firearm by Penal Code section 12021. Such conduct may be a felony and punishable by a $1,000 fine and imprisonment.*
- *Other violations of this order may also be felonies punishable by fines or imprisonment, or both.*

(Continued on reverse)

Form Adopted by Rule 1296.29
Judicial Council of California

RESTRAINING ORDER AFTER HEARING (CLETS)
(Domestic Violence Prevention)

Family Code § 6200 et seq

Restraining orders may offer some protection against stalkers. The names, addresses, and dates on this restraining order have been obscured.

police have also used harassment and antiterrorist statutes to curtail stalking, but such measures seldom help. Harassment laws generally carry only light penalties, while most antiterrorist statutes don't adequately apply to the stalker's behavior.

Roland Vaughn, past president of the International Association of Chiefs of Police, understands law enforcement's impotence with regard to stalking cases. He explains, "We're very limited in what we can do to preempt a violent crime. Usually we have to wait until one is committed."[1] Michigan State Senator R. Robert Geake, a nonpracticing psychologist, underscores these sentiments:

> A stalker's basic weapon is psychological terror, and our traditional legal structure does not adequately address that type of criminal activity. Stalking is probably as old as mankind. Its roots may go back to the ancient concept of women as property. A stalker wants to wield power over a woman. He's saying he's going to be part of her life, whether she likes it or not.[2]

The futility of existing legal measures against stalkers became graphically clear in 1990 when three California stalking cases ended tragically. Among these was that of thirty-two-year-old former Olympic skier Patricia Kastle, who was killed in Newport Beach, California, by a stalker against whom she had obtained a restraining order. Her death, and the stalking murders of two other California women by men against whom they had restraining orders, prompted state legislators to act. In September 1990, California passed the nation's first antistalking law, which defined a stalker as someone who "willfully, maliciously and repeatedly follows or harasses another person and makes a credible threat with the intent to place that person in reasonable fear of death or great bodily injury."[3] A convicted first offender may be sentenced to up to a year in a county jail, required to pay a fine of up to one thousand dollars, or both.

However, while Californians embarked on a road to curtail stalking, casualties resulting from the crime continued to mount across the nation. In Virginia Beach, Virginia, twenty-nine-year-old Regina Butkowski felt she had done everything possible to deter Parnell Jefferson, a weightlifter who stalked her after noticing the young woman at a health club. Butkowski changed apartments, screened all her telephone calls, and even had someone walk her to and from work, but Jefferson's fixation on her continued. The situation culminated tragically when he kidnapped Butkowski from her home and fatally shot her. He then set her corpse on fire and threw the body in a river. Parnell Jefferson was sentenced to life in prison.

West of where Regina Butkowski died, Milwaukee county bus driver Shirley Lowery was stalked by a former boyfriend who was obsessed with her. Like Butkowski, Lowery changed her residence, stopped going to church, and even hired bodyguards to protect her. Nevertheless, during her seventeen-month stalking ordeal, Lowery's former boyfriend raped her at gunpoint and eventually stabbed her to death at the Milwaukee County Courthouse in March 1993. Ironically, she had gone to the courthouse to get a restraining order against him.

In June 1992 in Georgia, Joyce Durden's estranged husband finally ended months of stalking by carrying out his repeated threats against her. He shot and killed the woman at a school where she taught mentally disturbed preschoolers, and then turned the gun on himself.

As the public is becoming increasingly aware of the pervasiveness and brutality of stalking, other states have begun to follow California's lead. By September

A federal judge issues a restraining order.
Difficulties in enforcing restraining orders
prevent them from offering complete security.
Usually, a stalking victim must take
additional safety measures.

1993, every state in the union and the District of Columbia had passed some form of antistalking legislation. While the various state laws often differ significantly, the National Victim Center has grouped them into the following three categories based on penalties:

1. Laws that make stalking a misdemeanor;
2. Laws that make the first stalking offense a misdemeanor and subsequent offenses felonies; and
3. Laws that make stalking a felony.[4]

The National Victim Center further notes that "most states [presently] classify the first-time stalking convictions as misdemeanors and subsequent convictions and/or violations of protective orders as felonies. A few states consider stalking a misdemeanor of varying degrees."[5]

In attempting to devise effective antistalking legislation, some states have adopted unique provisions. For example, Florida is the only state that permits police officers to arrest a suspected stalker without a warrant if there is reason to believe that a crime has occurred. Antistalking laws in Illinois, Hawaii, and Michigan permit the court to require counseling for stalkers, and Michigan offenders can be required to pay for this service themselves. In Iowa a stalker may be convicted of a "second" offense even if the second crime involves a different individual. The law specifies that the act of stalking be punished regardless of who the stalker focuses on.

While the new antistalking laws have merit, there are problems with some aspects of the legislation. In a number of instances, the constitutionality of the laws has been questioned. Civil liberty experts argue that much of the legislation is too vague and therefore has the potential for misuse. This could be especially troublesome in marital dispute cases. According to Miami criminal defense attorney Jeffrey Weiner, "There are very often false allegations made in all sorts of contexts against spouses or former spouses. For example, a woman might claim that her estranged husband has been threatening and harassing her and depending on the antistalking law in that state he could wind up in jail without bail until the time of his trial."[6]

There are other constitutionally troublesome questions. It has been argued that some antistalking legislation violates the due process clause of the Fourteenth Amendment to the Constitution, which requires that all laws be clearly and understandably written and fairly applied to the general population. It has been further noted that antistalking laws may infringe on an individual's right to travel and his First Amendment guarantee of free speech. Provisions that provide for a person's arrest without a warrant or detention without the possibility of bail are constitutionally questionable as well.

There may also be difficulties in applying the new legislation. For instance, there is inherent ambiguity in distinguishing a "credible threat" from a casual remark. Even when everyone involved is acting in good faith, a situation can be unsettling. As law professor Richard Allen puts it, "The idea behind stalking laws is to penalize threats. But what a threat is cannot be captured by a rule." Allen continues, "That invariably means comparing two people's points of view. A husband may say, 'Remember New Jersey?' Later he'll say he meant, 'Didn't we have a great time when we lived there?' But his wife thinks he meant, 'Remember the time I beat you?'"[7] There are often two sides to a story.

This concern came to the forefront in the case of George Martin-Trigona, who was accused of stalking a television anchorwoman for an extended period of time. Mr. Martin-Trigona claimed he was innocent and had been wrongfully labeled by the media and authorities. In describing his interaction with the anchorwoman, Martin-Trigona said, "I communicated with her intermittently over a two year period. I also stopped at the station and brought several books for her to read . . . and gave her some advice on journalism, to help her. And shortly thereafter I found myself slapped with this injunction."[8]

In underscoring his client's point, Martin-Trigona's attorneys added, "He [Martin-Trigona] never threatened this woman whatsoever. He's never done anything to harm this woman. I don't think that courting should be equated to stalking. I don't think that sending a letter should be equated [with stalking] . . . [someone] certainly shouldn't be imprisoned for something such as that."[9]

Yet just as the antistalking laws of numerous areas have been criticized by some for being unfairly inclusive, others argue that the legislation fails to adequately protect legitimate stalking victims. For example, Illinois requires that there either be two acts of harassment or that the stalker follow the person immediately after making a threat. But by the time a stalker's behavior has escalated to that level, it may be too late. As Lake County Chief Deputy State's Attorney Steven P. McCollum commented, "In real life the threat is the last thing that happens before the person is harmed."[10]

In Kansas, a person must be both harassed and followed for the stalker to be charged with a crime. This means that if a man follows a woman everywhere she goes, but fails to harass her in any other manner, he cannot be charged with stalking. Conversely, someone who sends a person a flood of annoying mail, or repeatedly harasses her or him by phone, is

In some states, a stalker cannot be charged with a crime unless the victim is both followed and harassed. Therefore, a stalker can legally watch a person twenty-four hours a day if he or she does not also harass the person.

not in violation of the antistalking law if the victim isn't also followed.

The Texas antistalking law specifies that following or otherwise harassing a person is only considered stalking after a victim has reported one such incident to the police. Therefore, a victim who initially doesn't take the situation seriously and waits several months before contacting law enforcement authorities will find that the offender's previous menacing behavior is disregarded.

A number of state statutes require that the victim fear "great bodily harm" from the stalker, which has been interpreted to mean that someone must believe the stalker is likely to "maim, disfigure, or kill" her or him to be protected under the law. This is of little help to a person whose life has been disrupted by a barrage of unpleasant phone calls and letters, but as yet has not been threatened with violence.

Still other state laws specify that the stalker must directly threaten the victim either verbally or in writing. This places the stalked individual in a difficult position because some offenders rely primarily on indirect or symbolic measures to terrorize their victims. In many cases this has included leaving small mutilated animals at the victim's door, sending the victim photographs of bloody corpses, or even sending bouquets of dead flowers.

Arguments regarding the constitutionality and effectiveness of the various state antistalking laws have been raised in both state legislatures and courts across America. Often, these court decisions are appealed at a higher level. In an effort to create more appropriate and nationally uniform legislation, in 1992 Congress directed the National Institute of Justice to devise a model antistalking law for the states that would "not be so broad as to be unconstitutional nor so narrow as to be virtually meaningless."[11]

Exactly what is a credible threat? Receiving a bouquet of dead flowers can be a powerful unspoken threat.

The end product of the Project to Develop a Model Antistalking Code for States was presented in October 1993. The task force offered a number of recommendations, which included making stalking a felony on the first offense instead of a misdemeanor as it presently is in most jurisdictions. It was also suggested that states impose stiffer penalties for the crime. It was extremely important to the task force that both the law enforcement community and the public at large acknowledge stalking as the hideous crime it often proves to be. "Unique to stalking," the report notes, "is the element of escalation that raises what initially may be bothersome and annoying—but legal—behavior to the level of the obsessive, dangerous, and even violent acts. Stalking victims, therefore, need to be provided with appropriate means to protect themselves against potential violence before it occurs."[12]

The project's director, Charles A. Lauer of the Justice Department's Office of Justice Programs stresses that the report largely concentrates on stalking incidents that perpetuate "a reasonable fear" of death or bodily harm. This distinguishes stalking from less serious crimes—such as telephone harassment, trespassing, or vandalizing property—that are covered under other laws. "We drew up a statute to say, 'This is stalking, folks, and nothing else,'" Lauer explains. "We feel that by making it very specific and differentiating it from other kinds of related violations, it will be used more. We don't want to confuse prosecutors by overlapping it with other crimes."[13]

Creators of the model antistalking law were comparably careful to avoid the "credible threat" wording found in many state laws. As a result, "threatening behavior" would not need to include an actual verbal or written threat to charge a stalker with a crime. To ensure the model law's constitutionality, broadly defined or vague terms such as "emotional distress," which could possibly compromise the rights of the accused, were deliberately avoided. The project's recommendations were provided to governors, state legislators, and District of Columbia officials, and a series of regional seminars was offered to encourage implementation of the recommendations. Following the model law's introduction, Wisconsin revamped its antistalking legislation, making it the first state to adopt major portions of the newly devised model law.

The enforceability of state antistalking laws was further boosted when President Bill Clinton signed the Violent Crime Control and Law Enforcement Act of 1994. The Act includes the Violence Against Women Act, which makes interstate stalking a federal offense.

Advances in antistalking legislation have been applauded by victims' rights groups throughout the nation. "A lot of [stalkers] are just caught up in the emotion of a bad break up," noted David Beatty of the National Victim Center in Arlington, Virginia. "Sitting someone down in jail for a while may make him rethink his actions."[14]

Others, however, question whether even well thought-out legislation can deter stalkers, especially those who are involved in obsessive love relationships or have serious psychological problems. According to clinical psychologist Stanton Samenow, a significant number of these individuals have distorted self-images that cause them to think that they are either models of excellence or worthless. Samenow feels that the stalker's intimidation ploys are merely a desperate effort to boost his self-esteem in response to the victim's rejection of him. Although threatening these individuals with imprisonment might sometimes be a deterrent, in other cases Samenow thinks it would be "like putting fuel on the fire."[15]

This gruesome prospect became evident several

weeks after Massachusetts passed its first antistalking law, when Susan [name changed], a nineteen-year-old student, was murdered by an ex-boyfriend turned stalker. Although Susan hadn't known it, her stalker had already spent nine months in jail for attacking another girlfriend. Nevertheless, she had gotten a restraining order against him when he began stalking her after their breakup.

But Susan's stalker never relented. Unable to let her go, he waited outside a store while she shopped, and when she left he repeatedly shot the young woman as she walked down the street. The stalker got away but was later found dead in his apartment after committing suicide. At his daughter's funeral, her father cynically remarked that the restraining order hadn't saved Susan and that the new law failed her as well.

Bianca [name changed], a twenty-six-year-old suburban Chicago homemaker, also doubts whether Illinois's antistalking legislation will stop her ex-husband. After attacking Bianca in an alley three years ago, he was convicted of aggravated battery. Since that time, he has spent fifteen months in jail, a year on parole, and five months on an electronic home monitoring program. Although he acquired 223 technical violations on the monitoring program, Bianca's former husband is now a free man. Bianca, who still has a misshapen nose and an eye injury from the beating, is uneasy about his possible access to her. "It's just a matter of when he feels like coming and getting me," she remarked.[16] Aware of his violent tendencies and past disregard for the law, the existence of a state antistalking statute has not eased Bianca's fears.

At times, law enforcement authorities have expressed similar frustrations in contending with persistent stalkers. They feel that the powers granted them by antistalking laws are still too limited. This is especially true in states that haven't yet revised their original legislation. "You can put a person in jail for a year or so, but they eventually will get out," laments a Los Angeles detective working on an antistalking unit.[17]

Many prosecutors feel similarly and cite stopping stalkers as one of the most difficult and frustrating tasks they face. "Unfortunately," notes Linda Fairstein, chief of the Sex Crimes Unit of New York City's Manhattan District Attorney's office, "it's not illegal for someone to join the same health club as you or sit in front of the building where you work, even if that means you have to walk past him every day to get to your job. Worse, these cases often aren't treated seriously," added Fairstein. "The first reaction is, 'What's the big deal?'. . . . [But] how do you predict which stalker is completely innocuous and which becomes the guy who shoots someone?"[18] While new antistalking legislation has undoubtedly been helpful in some cases, these laws may not be the ultimate solution to an insidious crime in which psychological terror is the offender's most valued weapon.

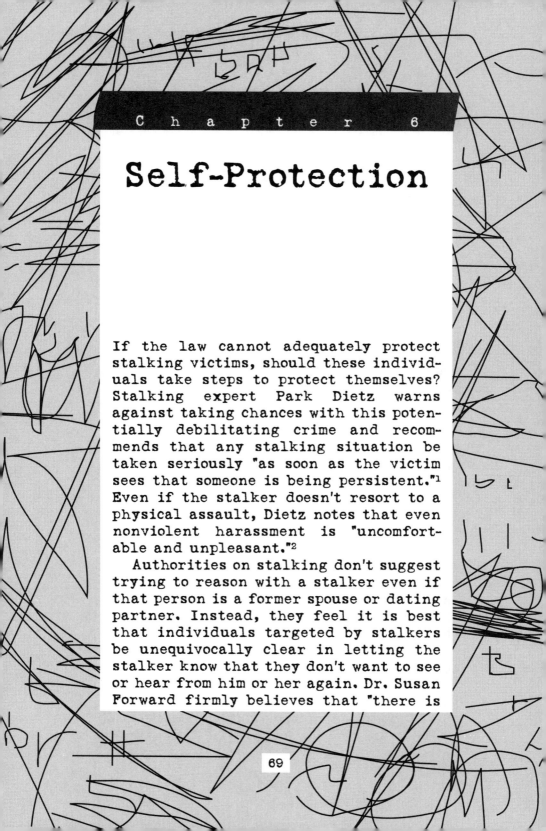

Self-Protection

If the law cannot adequately protect stalking victims, should these individuals take steps to protect themselves? Stalking expert Park Dietz warns against taking chances with this potentially debilitating crime and recommends that any stalking situation be taken seriously "as soon as the victim sees that someone is being persistent."[1] Even if the stalker doesn't resort to a physical assault, Dietz notes that even nonviolent harassment is "uncomfortable and unpleasant."[2]

Authorities on stalking don't suggest trying to reason with a stalker even if that person is a former spouse or dating partner. Instead, they feel it is best that individuals targeted by stalkers be unequivocally clear in letting the stalker know that they don't want to see or hear from him or her again. Dr. Susan Forward firmly believes that "there is no room for subtlety or uncertainty when trying to communicate with someone who doesn't want to hear what you're saying." Acknowledging that the assertive statements below "may seem harsh," Dr. Forward thinks that they "might [finally] get . . . [the stalker] to take [the] victim seriously."[3] Therefore, when appropriate, she advises stalking victims to use any of the following:

- It's over. This is not negotiable. I won't discuss it anymore.

- I'm going to hang up now, and if you call back I'll hang up again without speaking to you.

- I want you to leave now and I don't want you to come back. If you do, I won't let you in.

- Don't call, don't write, don't show up, don't contact me in any way.

- If you continue to harass me, I will have no choice but to get a court order against you.[4]

Dr. Forward adds that even though "explanations may make [the victim] feel less cruel . . . they can only muddy the waters, giving the obsessor hope that [the targeted person] can be persuaded to reconsider. An obsessor will never give up as long as [the victim is] still willing to talk."[5]

However, in cases in which stalking escalates to full-blown violence, the situation can become increasingly desperate. Verbally rebuffing the stalker may no longer be a consideration when the victim's safety is at risk. After assessing their circumstances, some stalking victims finally come to terms with a terrifying reality. Accepting that they may have to save themselves, they prepare to do so. That's how it was for Judith Ebelt, who had been stalked by her ex-husband for months. "Fear. I was so afraid, nobody knows," Ms. Ebelt recalls. "You're afraid to come home from work at night because he might be outside or something. . . . Every night that I came home from work I went through

70

Often, stalked individuals must fortify their houses with multiple locks to protect themselves.

the same routine of locking my doors—double locks on the doors and windows and everything."[6]

Though her ex-husband never threatened her life outright, Ebelt "believed it was going to come to that" and got a gun. The confrontation she dreaded occurred one night shortly thereafter when her ex-husband armed himself and crashed through her door to enter Ebelt's home. She shot him before he could kill her.

Twenty-seven-year-old Sonia (name changed) began carrying a gun after she had been stalked for several months by a coworker and had filed numerous ineffective police complaints. In June 1992, when the stalker trapped her in a parking lot and tried to force her into her car with him, she pulled out the handgun and shot him twice in the stomach. After being hospitalized, the stalker was charged with attempted kidnapping. Sonia was never charged with a crime. In commenting on why no action was taken against her, a detective on the case said, "I don't think you would find a jury in Texas that would convict her, so why try?"[7]

Despite these examples, law enforcement authorities do not recommend that individuals being stalked arm themselves with guns. In their book *Stalked: Breaking the Silence on the Crime of Stalking in America*, authors Melita Schaum and Karen Parrish suggest that a stalking victim who is contemplating securing a weapon carefully weigh the following concerns before deciding to do so:

- An intruder may use it against you;
- Most people hesitate to shoot an intruder; and
- There is the potential for a tragic accident with a gun in the home, particularly if children are present.[8]

Yet there are numerous other measures available to stalked individuals to help them protect themselves and cope with the crisis at hand. These include the following.

Be Informed

Because a stalker largely relies on terrorizing the victim and having her or him feel helpless, knowing as much as possible about available resources can go a long way in making a stalked person feel in control as well as possibly diffusing an explosive situation. A free copy of any state's antistalking law can be readily obtained by either writing or calling the local district attorney (prosecutor) or the state's attorney general's office. As state laws still widely vary, it is vital that the stalking victim read and understand the applicable legislation so the person knows precisely when the stalker has technically violated the law. If any portion of the statute is difficult to comprehend, the district attorney's office can provide an explanation for clarification.

Some victim support groups further encourage stalking victims to learn as much as possible about related laws, such as those dealing with harassment, trespassing, and vandalism. This knowledge can be crucial in stalking cases because victims who know their rights are better able to determine precisely when these rights have been violated or infringed upon.

Work with Law Enforcement Personnel

Once a stalker has broken the law, the victim should immediately report the incident to the police. Whenever this occurs, it is wise to request a copy of the police report and file it away for possible future reference.

At times, police have been reluctant to file reports on stalking incidents, categorizing these episodes as domestic disputes that rarely result in criminal convictions. Michigan lawyer Lee Williams suggests a controversial way of dealing with law enforcement officials. "If you want the system to take you seriously," he advises, "you're better off not telling the truth if it's your ex-husband or ex-boyfriend stalking you. Tell the police it's a man you've never met."[9]

Actually, lying is probably not the best way to

Stalking victims should not hesitate to
report incidents to the police.

deal with the police. Even though it may be frustrating at times, it is essential for anyone being stalked to be direct and honest in their dealings with law enforcement officials. Many of the antistalking laws are still fairly new or in the process of being revised, so some police officers may not be very knowledgeable about them. Therefore, it is sometimes up to the victims to point out how the legislation applies to their case. If an officer is still hesitant to file a report on a stalking incident, politely ask to see his or her supervisor and repeat your request.

Let the Stalker Know You Have Taken Legal Action to Curtail the Harassment

The National Victim Center advises stalked individuals to do the following:

> Have law enforcement officials notify the stalker to stop the action. . . . Obtain a protective or restraining order that requires the offender to cease contact with you. These orders are obtained by filing forms with the prosecutor's office, a local court or magistrate.[10]

The Center warns victims, however, that "a protective order is just a piece of paper that may be readily ignored by the stalker."[11] Genuine security requires more than a court order.

Involve Others

Taking further protective measures frequently involves making people in the victim's life aware of what is happening and what they can do to help. While some people, fearing the stalker's retaliation, may initially resist involvement, eventually the victim should

establish a solid base of support. Friends may escort the victim to and from work and accompany the victim while shopping or doing errands.

If this isn't always possible, stalked individuals should routinely vary their schedules and routes to make it difficult for the stalker to know their whereabouts at particular times. Stalking victims who must drive either to work or class should consider getting a car phone. This enables them to call for help if they spot the stalker following them.

Ideally, neighbors should be given either a photograph or a detailed description of the stalker to enable them to immediately alert the police if the offender is seen on or near the premises. It may also help to provide neighbors with the license number and a description of the stalker's vehicle. If the victim is employed or goes to school, the company's security staff or school administration should also be alerted to the problem in the event that the stalker appears at the site.

If possible, stalking victims should make certain that someone close to them always knows where they are and when they are expected home. Some victims have found it especially helpful to have friends or relatives call their home at prearranged times on evenings and weekends in case the stalker has broken in and the victim can't call for help. By mentioning a previously agreed upon code word, the victim can signal the caller to notify the police without the stalker knowing.

> Being accompanied by a friend when going to or from work or school may deter a stalker from approaching.

Keep Accurate and
Detailed Records

Victims should write down each interchange with the stalker. These records should include a brief description of what happened along with the date, time, and place it occurred. If there were witnesses, their names, addresses, and phone numbers should be noted as well. Photographs depicting how the stalker vandalized or otherwise damaged the victim's property are also useful. This type of documentation can be a key factor in building a solid case against the stalker and effectively involving law enforcement officials.

Have a Prearranged Escape Plan

Unfortunately, stalking victims need to be prepared for crisis situations that may occur without warning. Experts recommend that stalked individuals always carry some extra money with them in case it becomes necessary to jump into a cab or on a bus or train while eluding a pursuer. Stalking victims who drive should always keep their car's gas tank filled.

Keeping some change handy in a pocket or separate coin purse enables the victim to quickly make a phone call in an emergency. Stalked individuals should also carry a list of important phone numbers with them. These numbers might include those of the victim's attorney, a police detective on the case, a woman's shelter (if the stalked person is female), and family members capable of providing crisis assistance.

Practice Car and Home Security

Stalked individuals need to take special precautions to prevent the offender from entering their vehicle and home. This entails keeping their car doors locked and windows up at all times, as well as parking in well-lit, busy areas. Prior to entering their cars, stalking victims should check fully both inside and under the vehicle to insure that the stalker isn't lurking there.

Stalking victims should always lock the doors and windows of their homes and garages, and they should keep their blinds or curtains drawn. Preferably, dead bolt locks should be installed on doors leading outside, and if feasible, an alarm system should be installed. Some people who have been stalked have found that a guard dog can alert them to intruders as well as any costly alarm system. If the stalking victim resides in a private home, the exterior should be well-lit. It is essential that any shrubbery surrounding the house be well maintained—some stalkers have hidden behind bushes and hedges while spying on or sneaking up on their victims.

ADT Security Systems has been working on a personal alarm system that could be of value to stalking victims. In this system, those being stalked wear a pendant around their necks. If they see the stalker, they press the pendant and an ADT monitoring system alerts the police. The system seems promising, but there are some drawbacks. Presently, the pendant is only functional within range of the victim's home where a signal receiving device has been installed. Another potential problem is that the system depends on phone lines, which could be cut by a determined stalker.

The system was tested by six female residents of Tampa, Florida, who had previously stayed at the Spring Women's Shelter after having been stalked and battered by their former husbands and boyfriends. While all the women wore the pendant for six months, only one used it when her ex-husband unexpectedly arrived at her home threatening to kill her. Although the police intervened in time, the woman was so shaken by the incident that she returned the pendant and went underground to hide from her former spouse.

A dog determined to protect its owner may
sometimes temporarily scare off a stalker.

Maintain Your Emotional
and Physical Well Being

Stalking victims frequently experience stress and
depression resulting from the offender's threats and
harassment. During this ongoing nightmare, those

who have been stalked often report sleep distur-
bances, eating problems, and mood swings in addition to numerous other symptoms that typify emotional
distress.

At times, establishing a strong support network
may be essential to the person's emotional well being
and ultimate survival. This means not listening to
people who tend to blame the victim for the situation
or habitually minimize the stalker's actions. One stalking victim explains what facing these attitudes is like:

> Friends and coworkers don't understand the se-
> riousness of it. My mom can't comprehend it. My
> dad says ignore it. I've had people say "He just
> really loves you." My own boss told me at one
> point . . . that he didn't know who was the liar [the
> stalker] or me! . . . I was fuming mad.[12]

Another stalking victim echos these sentiments. Not-
ing the kinds of reactions she received, she recalls:

> The most valuable support I got was validation of
> my fear—an empathy about why the actions of
> the stalker were frightening. Most damaging
> were those who minimized by saying, "He hasn't
> really done anything."[13]

The National Victim Center stresses that stalking victims "have done nothing to invite this behavior. The
stalker is the one who is wrong."[14] Besides relying on
family members, friends, and coworkers for support,
the Center suggests that individuals who are stalked
should "not hesitate to seek the assistance of [a] professional counselor . . . [during] this emotional
trauma."[15] It hopes that those going through this crisis
will "always remember [that] victims can become
survivors."[16]

Epilogue

Some regard the recent sweep of anti-stalking legislation as proof that the crime is finally being taken seriously. Yet while stalking is now readily condemned, in some ways society still may tacitly encourage behavior that leads to stalking crimes.

Very young children grow up hearing fairy tales in which knights and princes bravely battle dragons and witches to win the princess. Giving up would be considered unmanly. Later on, these children see television shows, films, and magazine advertisements that glamorize heated romantic pursuit. In romantic comedies, the persistent suitor often refuses to give up, even if he must kidnap or assault the girl to win out.

Romantic pursuit is such an integral part of dating that even works that are intended to be sinister are often viewed as innocent love stories by society at large. In 1983, the rock band The Police released the song "Every Breath You Take," containing the lyrics:

> Every breath you take
> Every move you make
> Every bond you break
> Every step you take
> I'll be watching you.[1]

Though the band intended the song to be from the point of view of an obsessed stalker, most listeners perceived it as a tender love song. Few people thought twice about dedicating it to their loved-ones on the radio.

Clearly, most romantic pursuit is innocent. Problems may arise, however, when boys are taught that women really mean yes when they say no—these women, they are told, may be "playing hard to get." These boys may mistakenly believe that females respect and admire men who forcefully take them despite their protests. They can easily find apparent affirmation of this misconception in the popular media; it is not uncommon to see women in films surrender in ecstasy after first trying to break free from the man's embrace.

Youths are continually taught the value of persistence in academic, sporting, or romantic endeavors. There's even a perfume called Obsession. But when an obsessed lover won't accept rejection and feels that "all's fair in love and war," the distinction between acceptable pursuit and violence may blur.

Many stalkers are individuals involved in unhealthy obsessive relationships. They don't realize that obsessive or all-consuming love isn't really love at all, and unlike in the films they have seen, it is bound to end unhappily. As Dr. Susan Forward explains, "Obsessive love . . . is dominated by fear, possessiveness and jealousy. Obsessive love is volatile and sometimes even dangerous. Ultimately, it never satisfies, never nourishes, and it rarely feels good."[2]

Perhaps the answer at least partially lies in young people hearing a new message encouraging them to develop a positive self-image and accept appropriate boundaries in their relationships. Can the next generation free itself from the stereotypes embraced by the present one? In the end, romantic partnerships soundly based on equality and mutual respect may be more effective in curtailing stalking than any legislation.

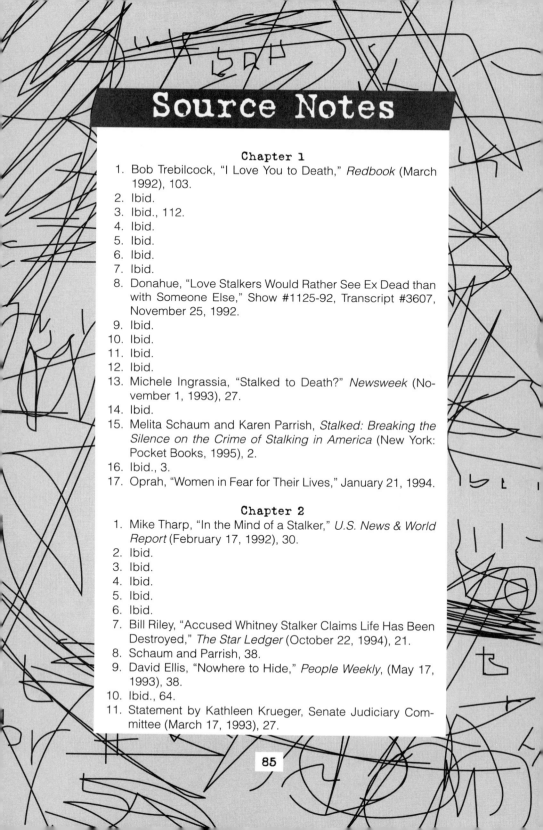

Source Notes

Chapter 1

1. Bob Trebilcock, "I Love You to Death," *Redbook* (March 1992), 103.
2. Ibid.
3. Ibid., 112.
4. Ibid.
5. Ibid.
6. Ibid.
7. Ibid.
8. Donahue, "Love Stalkers Would Rather See Ex Dead than with Someone Else," Show #1125-92, Transcript #3607, November 25, 1992.
9. Ibid.
10. Ibid.
11. Ibid.
12. Ibid.
13. Michele Ingrassia, "Stalked to Death?" *Newsweek* (November 1, 1993), 27.
14. Ibid.
15. Melita Schaum and Karen Parrish, *Stalked: Breaking the Silence on the Crime of Stalking in America* (New York: Pocket Books, 1995), 2.
16. Ibid., 3.
17. Oprah, "Women in Fear for Their Lives," January 21, 1994.

Chapter 2

1. Mike Tharp, "In the Mind of a Stalker," *U.S. News & World Report* (February 17, 1992), 30.
2. Ibid.
3. Ibid.
4. Ibid.
5. Ibid.
6. Ibid.
7. Bill Riley, "Accused Whitney Stalker Claims Life Has Been Destroyed," *The Star Ledger* (October 22, 1994), 21.
8. Schaum and Parrish, 38.
9. David Ellis, "Nowhere to Hide," *People Weekly*, (May 17, 1993), 38.
10. Ibid., 64.
11. Statement by Kathleen Krueger, Senate Judiciary Committee (March 17, 1993), 27.

12. Ibid.
13. Ibid., 28
14. Schaum and Parrish, 41.
15. David Ellis, "Bloody Obsessions," *People Weekly* (May 10, 1993), 71.
16. Stanley Holmes, "Open to Attack; for Women Athletes, a Fear of Stalking," *Newsweek* (January 17, 1994), 46.
17. Ibid., 47.
18. Ibid., 46.
19. Ibid.
20. Ibid.

Chapter 3
1. Sally Jessy Raphael, "He Was After Me," Transcript #1633, January 9, 1994.
2. Ibid.
3. Oprah, "Women in Fear for Their Lives."
4. Dr. Susan Forward, *Obsessive Love: When It Hurts Too Much to Let Go* (New York: Bantam Books, 1991), 23.
5. Oprah, "Women in Fear for Their Lives."
6. Oprah, "Obsession, When Passion Holds You Prisoner," May 29, 1991.
7. Forward, 19.
8. Oprah, "Obsession."
9. Schaum and Parrish, 65.

Chapter 4
1. Sally Jessy Raphael, "I'm Too Young to Be Stalked," Transcript #1602, October 27, 1994.
2. Ibid.
3. Ibid.
4. Ibid.
5. Ibid.
6. Claire Safron, "A Stranger Was Stalking Our Little Girl," *Good Housekeeping* (November 1992), 264.

Chapter 5
1. Howard Kohn, "The Stalker," *Redbook* (April 1993), 130.
2. Ibid.
3. Ibid.
4. National Victim Center, "Stalking," *Infolink,* vol. 1, no. 63, 1994, 2.
5. Ibid.
6. Melinda Beck, "Murderous Obsession," *Newsweek* (July 13, 1992), 61.

7. Ibid.
8. Donahue, "Lover Stalkers Would Rather See Ex Dead than with Someone Else," Show #1125-92, Transcript #3607, November 25, 1992.
9. Ibid.
10. Schaum and Parrish, 172.
11. Senator William Cohen's Proposed Federal Stalking Statute: Hearing before the Senate Committee of the Judiciary. 103d Congress, 1st Session, 1993.
12. George Lardner, Jr., "Federal Task Force Suggests Making Stalking a Felony Offense," *Washington Post* (September 12, 1993), A19.
13. Ibid.
14. Beck, "Murderous Obsession."
15. Ibid.
16. Michele Ingrassia, "Stalked to Death," *Newsweek* (November 1, 1993), 28.
17. Beck, "Murderous Obsession."
18. Bob Trebilcock, "Can You Stop a Stalker?" *Redbook* (March 1992), 114.

Chapter 6

1. Trebilcock, 114.
2. Ibid.
3. Forward, 158.
4. Ibid.
5. Ibid.
6. Oprah, "Women In Fear for Their Lives," January 21, 1994.
7. Beck, "Murderous Obsession."
8. Schaum and Parrish, 130.
9. Howard Kohn, "The Stalker," *Redbook* (April 1993), 130.
10. National Victim Center, "Stalking," *Infolink*, vol. 1, no. 63, 1994, 2.
11. Ibid.
12. Schaum and Parrish, 108.
13. Ibid.
14. National Victim Center, 5.
15. Ibid.
16. Ibid.

Epilogue

1. Sting, "Every Breath You Take," *Synchronicity*, The Police, A & M Records CS-3735.
2. Forward, 10.

Related Organizations

AMEND
777 Grant St., Ste. 600
Denver, CO 80203

AMERICAN SECURITY COUNCIL
Washington Communications Center
Boston, VA 22713
(703) 547-1776

BATTERERS ANONYMOUS
8485 Tamarind, Ste. D
Fontana, CA 92335

EMERGE: COUNSELING AND EDUCATION TO STOP MALE VIOLENCE
18 Hurley St. , Ste. 100
Cambridge, MA 02141

NATIONAL ASSAULT PREVENTION CENTER
P.O. Box 02005
Columbus, OH 43202

NATIONAL COALITION AGAINST DOMESTIC VIOLENCE
P.O. Box 18749
Denver, CO 80218

NATIONAL COUNCIL ON CHILD ABUSE AND FAMILY VIOLENCE
1155 Connecticut Ave., NW, Ste. 400
Washington, DC 20036

NATIONAL ORGANIZATION FOR VICTIM ASSISTANCE
1757 Park Rd. NW
Washington, DC 20010
(800) TRY-NOVA or (202) 232-6682

NATIONAL ORGANIZATION FOR WOMEN
100 16th Street NW, Ste. 700
Washington, DC 20036
(202) 331-0066

NATIONAL VICTIM CENTER
307 W. 7th Street, Ste. 1001
Fort Worth, TX 76102
(817) 877-3355

WOMEN IN CRISIS
133 W. 21st St., 11th Fl.
New York, NY 10011
(212) 242-4880

Internet Resources

Because of the changeable nature of the Internet, sites appear and disappear very quickly. These resources offered useful information on stalking at the time of publication. Internet addresses must be entered with capital and lowercase letters exactly as they appear.

Yahoo:
http://www.yahoo.com/
The Yahoo directory of the World Wide Web is an excellent place to find Internet sites on any topic.

Survivors Of Stalking, Inc.:
http://www.gate.net/~soshelp/
Survivors Of Stalking, Inc. (S.O.S.) is a nonprofit, volunteer organization dedicated to providing support for stalking victims and their families, as well as heightening public awareness of the crime. All services and assistance are provided free of charge to victims and their family members.

FindLaw:
http://www.findlaw.com/
FindLaw is dedicated to providing legal information on the Internet. Information regarding antistalking laws can be found through this site.

The Domestic Violence Information Pages:
http://www.iquest.net/~gtemp/domvi.htm
The Domestic Violence Information Pages contain the following types of information about domestic violence:
- essays and comments;
- facts;
- hotline numbers;
- family services contacts;
- Web site links; and
- a suggested reading list.

The National Institute of Justice:
http://www.ncjrs.org/nijhome.htm

The National Institute of Justice (NIJ), a component of the Office of Justice Programs, is the research and development agency of the U.S. Department of Justice. NIJ was established to prevent and reduce crime and to improve the criminal justice system. As part of its Project to Develop a Model Antistalking Code for States, NIJ published guidelines in an effort to make local antistalking laws more uniform and appropriate. The NIJ Web site offers much information regarding stalking and other crimes. You may request a free copy of the Project to Develop a Model Antistalking Code for States report by calling the National Criminal Justice Association at (202) 347-4900 or writing them at 444 North Capitol Street NW, Suite 618, Washington, DC 20001.

Further Reading

Braiker, Harriet. *Lethal Lovers and Poisonous People*. New York: Pocket Books, 1992.

Dvorchak, Robert J. *Someone Is Stalking Me*. New York: Dell, 1993.

Forward, Susan. *Obsessive Love: When It Hurts Too Much to Let Go*. New York: Bantam Books, 1991.

Gross, Linda. *To Have or To Harm: True Stories of Stalkers and Their Victims*. New York: Warner Books, 1994.

Markman, Ronald. *Obsessed: The Stalking of Theresa Saldana*. New York: Morrow, 1994.

Porterfield, Kay Marie. *Violent Voices: 12 Steps to Freedom form Verbal and Emotional Abuse*. Deerfield Beach: Health Communications, 1989.

Skalias, Lavonne. *Stalked: A True Story*. Fort Worth: Summit Group, 1994.

Swisher, Karin and Wekesser, Carol, Eds. *Violence Against Women*. San Diego: Greenhaven Press, 1994.

United States Congress Senate Committee on the Judiciary, Antistalking Legislation: Hearing before the Committee on the Judiciary, United States Senate, One Hundred Second Congress. Washington, D.C.: U.S. G.P.O., 1993.

United States Congress Senate Committee on the Judiciary, Antistalking Proposals: Hearing before the Committee on the Judiciary, United States Senate, One Hundred Third Congress. Washington, D.C.: U.S. G.P.O., 1993.

Index

Italicized page numbers indicate illustrations.

About the Author

Popular author Elaine Landau worked as a newspaper reporter, an editor, and a youth services librarian before becoming a full-time writer. She has written more than ninety nonfiction books for young people, including *Tuberculosis* and *We Have AIDS*. Ms. Landau, who has a bachelor's degree in English and journalism from New York University and a master's degree in library and information science from Pratt Institute, lives in New Jersey with her husband and son.